IRMA-GEDDON: 2017
The Gift of Tragedy

As documented by
Happy GoLucky and the Resilient Community of
Marathon, Florida Keys

ISBN-13:
978-1978442207

ISBN-10:
1978442203

First Edition: December 2017

The Gift of Tragedy

"Category 4 Irma hit the Florida Keys beginning on 9/9/2017 and stayed here way too long. We got whacked Big Time."

Happy GoLucky

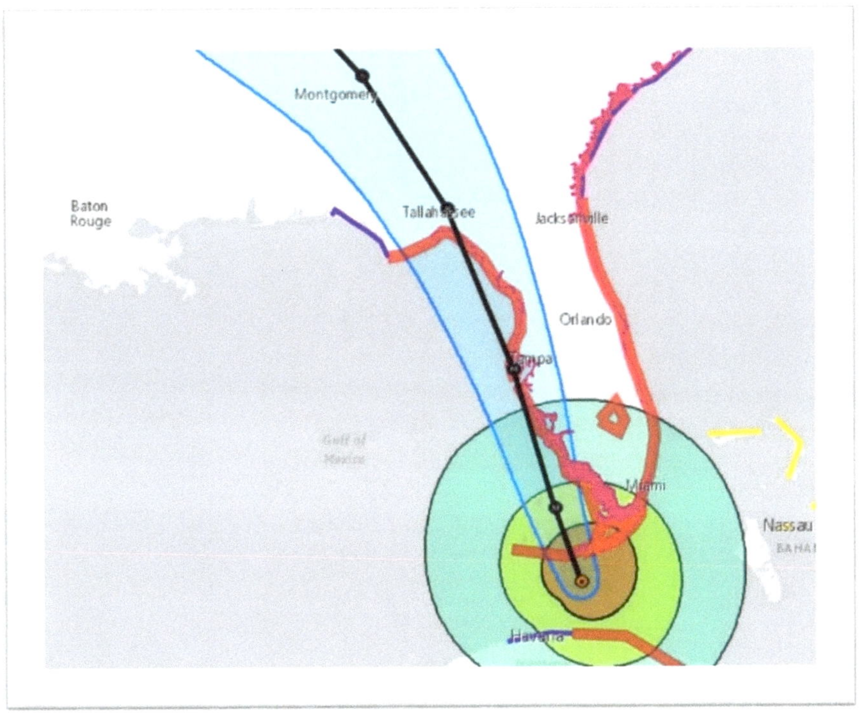

The Gift of Tragedy

The Gift of Tragedy

This poignant diary written with amazing grace, humor and love by a man in Marathon, Florida Keys, captures in full verbal color the deep reaching spirit of a community broken to bits by the ravages of Hurricane Irma that hit September 9, 2017.

With the enormous power of words, sweat, aching muscles, giving more than anyone knew they could give and most of all, Big Love, "The Gift of Tragedy" is a moving, honest, insightful account of the strength of 'average people' recovering from the unimaginable.

Meet "Happy GoLucky" and his dedicated Florida Keys community who, with resolve, determination, and hope, began rebuilding their homes, healing their souls and on extra exhausting days, didn't forget to wear their pants.

The Gift of Tragedy

This book is published by Ingram Books, Fall City, WA and is available for a not-for-profit price at the largest, most well-known online book retailer whose "jungle" name cannot be legally mentioned in this publication.

The Gift of Tragedy

IRMA-GEDDON
September, 2017
Marathon, Florida Keys

Happy GoLucky

September 10 ·

To all my dear friends: After a long break, returning to Facebook to reach out. This is S. & ML who live in Marathon, FL. We want you to know we are safe in Georgia. We are waiting for news from home. I send love and prayers to my friends in and of the Keys, and my heartfelt gratitude for all the love and assistance from people everywhere.

Happy GoLucky

September 12 ·

We left cars at the house. It may appear we are inside and they will force locks to look for bodies. If anyone knows who we can contact to prevent the locks on elevator from being forced, this would be greatly appreciated. If those locks are compromised the elevator will be inoperable and it will set back any hope we have for recovery a great deal. Thanks for any help you can provide.

Happy GoLucky

September 12 ·

Read a post that said Bz Z. and Amy, their bar "The Salty Angler" in Key West and their house are all good.

Happy GoLucky

September 14 ·

First look at flyover I was feeling optimistic. Some roof damage was evident, but mostly ok. Today, I looked carefully at photo. Appears that elevator shaft toppled into house. This is a MAJOR setback. 😟 :(

Happy GoLucky

September 14 ·

Eager to see with these eyes the true condition of my home. Need to be patient until then. What will be will be. But whatever I find, it will all be ok in the end. My thoughts are with all affected by Irma.

Happy GoLucky

September 15 at 10:31am ·

Just received photos of the condition of our home. Elevator shaft is fine, no flooding, no major damage visible anywhere. Definitely some work & repairs ahead, but we feel blessed. Our thoughts and prayers remain with all who are affected by Irma. We will all be ok because we will help each other. Our heartfelt gratitude for all the love & support from folks everywhere.

At the same time, down in Key West and against all warnings, The Salty Angler owners stayed through Hurricane Irma and opened their doors to the public as soon as humanly possible. They served endless free meals to the locals and provided the community with a place to meet and share. Musicians and bartenders volunteered their time and talents. Below is just a small example of the heartfelt community support The Salty Angler and Friends provided for the locals and the stranded in the Key West.

Meanwhile, back in the Middle Keys…

Happy GoLucky
September 16 at 9:42am ·
OK, the desperately wondering part is over. Enough communication has been restored that we have a good idea of where things stand. Some fared relatively well, some got hit hard. But most everyone stayed alive. Much work has been done. There's so much work to do. Let's get to it. Our friend Harry said it best; "there's no "me" now, only "we." WE will do the work that needs done. Help your brothers & sisters. Let them help you. I love you all.

Happy GoLucky
September 20 at 9:16am ·

Marathon - YOU ARE FREAKIN' AWESOME! 

Happy GoLucky
September 23 at 4:59am ·
Got home yesterday. We've got work to do. Grateful. Thank you, friends.

Happy GoLucky
September 23 at 5:14am ·
Water is Life. Good News! Boil Water Advisory for Marathon has been lifted.

Happy GoLucky
September 24 at 7:09am ·
"Many hands make light work."

No one can do everything, but everyone can do something. Help where you can, do what you can. Lend a hand.

Happy GoLucky

September 24 at 7:15am ·

Put on your own oxygen mask before assisting others, but once you are breathing properly, help your fellow travelers.

Happy GoLucky

September 24 at 7:21am ·

I am in awe of the many displays of courage, selflessness, charity, kindness and love that I've witnessed during this truly catastrophic disaster. People Rock.

Happy GoLucky

September 24 at 10:40am ·

Feeling good, but a little beat up. Gonna take a break and watch some Sunday football and see Deli at the Ale House. I'll be there at 1:00 p.m. Come say hi!

Happy GoLucky

September 25 at 6:04am ·

Yesterday was a nice break. Today the work continues and intensifies. The dwelling is dried in and we have most of the creature comforts. Now it's time to start putting order to chaos. So much to do. If you have a hand to spare, hit me up. 🩷🖤

Happy GoLucky

September 25 at 2:28pm ·

Nephew Chris drove 1600 miles since Friday night to lend a hand in our Irma recovery. Arrived yesterday morning. He stopped at South of the Border and brought big sombrero's.

Happy GoLucky

September 25 at 8:26pm ·

Great Day of Irma recovery activities. Chris, Mary Lou, Cornelia H., Katy K., neighbor Matt & I kicked butt. Plenty left to do, but such improvement. Crew was stellar. Words just can't express our gratitude.

Happy GoLucky

September 26 at 7:18am ·

I've had my share of challenges in my life, and, for the most part, I've met the call. Not much scares me or gets to me. When I felt we had lost our house, I figured it would be a new beginning. But what makes me cry like a baby is the generosity, love, charity and caring showered on us during this catastrophe. Y'all found my weak spot and you keep hitting it over and over. I love you.

Happy GoLucky

September 27 at 3:32am ·

So nice to see my neighbors and friends (and myself) knitting our lives and our community back together. We make progress each day. Long road ahead, but I'm happy to be traveling it with amazing companions.

Happy GoLucky

September 27 at 9:30am ·

OK. Enough dicking around on FB. Can't avoid it any longer. Sore or not, get up and do it again.

Happy GoLucky

September 27 at 10:21pm ·

Today kicked my ass. The fatigue is cumulative from the first day Irma became a serious threat. But, you know what? WE ARE KEYS STRONG! And so are YOU! We got this! Just tell me what day it is.

Happy GoLucky
September 28 at 5:27am ·

Here comes a new dawn. Here comes a new day. Tune up, start to play. Just like every other day. Love you babies. Stay Strong. ❤🖤

The Gift of Tragedy

IRMA-GEDDON
OCTOBER, 2017
Marathon, Florida Keys

Happy GoLucky
October 1 at 3:42am ·
Stopped by DRC for a brief visit yesterday. Some relatively minor damage, but looks functional. Dolphins were talkative.

Happy GoLucky
October 1 at 3:45am ·
Up most of the night, but nothing new about that. Body sore, but not screaming. Grateful for the return to "regular" feelings. Not quite there, but close.

Happy GoLucky

October 1 at 3:58am ·

Driving around Marathon & Grassy Key yesterday, I was in awe of how much has been accomplished in a short three weeks. Also startled by the intensity of the damage and the enormity of the impact on our community. This is one time we should be glad that we live in a place far from normal. It's going to take all of us being Keys Strong for as long as it takes. The healing has begun, keep it going, babies. You see somebody winding down, lift them up. We need everybody. No one left behind. ❤️🖤

Happy GoLucky

October 3 at 2:57am ·

Blue Monday. Tragedy dominates the news. It rained hard this Tuesday morning. As I often do, I awoke in the wee hours hoping it was closer to sunrise. I can't wait to smell coffee and see the sun. I want this night to be over. I want a new day with all the promise it brings. I know every cloud has a silver lining. But some days it's hard to be cheery without feeling like a fool. But what's the alternative? So, let me be your cheery fool. Together we will find a way to survive this shit show. We will know joy. I love you. For real.

Happy GoLucky

October 3 at 7:30am ·

Something I noticed just now; everyone who follows me on Facebook is a leader in real life. Mad Respect.

Happy GoLucky

October 3 at 7:36am ·

Coffee and sunshine. Life is good. Best Day Ever. 

Happy GoLucky

October 3 at 8:49am ·

In the good news department, Yesterday, Emily H. , Mary Lou & I were able to raise a couple knocked down trees. They look like they have a good chance of living. Each one is a lot of work, but we're going to save all that are savable. Many more to do. Each time we raise a tree, it gets easier to move around and clear debris. It gets better each day.

Happy GoLucky

October 4 at 6:56am ·

Dear Friends, three years ago I suspended my Facebook account with no prior notice. I reactivated the account in response to Hurricane Irma, I've enjoyed my time here, seeing all of you that are so dear to me. The disaster information and support has been invaluable. The social connections are a godsend. However, I find myself getting caught by many of the same energy sinks that caused me to suspend my account in 2014. I intend to stick around for a bit, Irma recovery isn't far enough along that I feel comfortable putting down this valuable tool. But I will go when the time is right. Just don't want to do it as abruptly this time as last. I love you all and I don't want to be the source of any confusion you might experience when you don't find me here. ❤🖤

Happy GoLucky

October 5 at 5:37am ·

Good Morning, Babies! Today is Thursday, October 5, 2017. It's approaching 5:00 a.m. As is my habit, I spent the night alternating between a half hour of sleep and an hour of stupefied wakens. It rained most of the night. Mostly showers, with occasional wind gusts and driving rain. Lost Comcast internet for a while. The tv service stayed up.

Yesterday was a good day. <u>Emily H.</u> and I started late and quit early, but accomplished our goal of cleaning up a corner of the yard. Trimmed some trees and picked up and hauled storm debris consisting primarily of tree limbs, palm fronds, coconuts and roof shingles.

We sat down to a wonderful supper prepared by the incomparable ML. A dear friend and neighbor also graced us with her company.

Not yet sure where the day will take me. The weather may put a halt to outdoor cleanup. I'll fill up with caffeine and sort the priorities. We're closing in on a month since the storm hit. Progress has been remarkable. What remains to be done is awesome in scope. Folks are beginning to get a more realistic sense of what lies ahead. Some will decide that the hill is just too steep and load their wagon with whatever they can carry to greener pastures. I know how much they want to stay, and my heart breaks for them. The rest of us see just how long this road to recovery stretches out ahead. Here's the part where I talk about how strong we are. I do so without any sense of it being bullshit. Everybody is beat up and tired, but I'm confident that we will rally. I know the people who live on these rocks. I will go to war with them anytime. We got this! Everybody wants to know what they can send to help in the recovery. For me personally, I need helping hands, good vibes, and some funny jokes. If you happen to hit the lottery . . . just break me off a little sompin'. But mostly, just keep loving us down here and keep letting us feel your love. ❤️🖤❤️
🖤

Happy GoLucky

October 6 at 5:36am ·

TGIF? TGFC! (thank g 4 coffee). Some sleep last night, about the usual. Kinda sore from yesterday's yard work. Hardest part is maneuvering over roots and rocks. Fortunate to still be able to do the work. <u>Emily H.</u> and I are making headway. We got more storm debris picked up and hauled to the street. If you aren't here, it's difficult to imagine the volume of refuse at hand. Emily fixed the catch on the screen door that was banging in the wind before we tied it shut with rope. Maybe someday soon we can start replacing the porch screens. Speaking of the back porch, it's our favorite space. We spend most of our time there. It used to be very private because of being surrounded by trees. Post storm - "Howdy Neighbors." Nothing stays the same. I see privacy screen in my future. Not because I don't like my neighbors, I certainly do. But drinking morning coffee out back after a shower used to require no more than a towel for covering. Now, that would turn into a "Friend's" episode starring the "naked, fat guy."

Happy GoLucky

October 6 at 6:21am ·

The shock factor of Irma is wearing off. I'm beginning to be cognizant of the name of the current day. Along with that adjustment comes the certainty that there is SO much to do to get our town beyond this disaster. The piles of debris are unimaginable. Seeing isn't believing. The scale is beyond belief. Businesses are making heroic efforts to serve customers. Most are short staffed, under supplied, working to make repairs to their buildings and grounds . . . and many still have to go home to face major disruption of their personal lives. PLEASE BE KIND TO OUR BUSINESS COMMUNITY. Be patient. They are us.

Happy GoLucky

October 7 at 4:59pm ·

Another day of yard work. Emily H., neighbor Gary, ML & I made some headway. A nice Pigeon Plum tree uplifted successfully. More yard debris cleared. Talked with my roofer neighbor; they have ordered satellite views of my roof in order to prepare an estimate. Evidently, these photos are so accurate they are used to measure and cut metal roofing ready to install. Who knew? These women are remarkable neighbors who are coping with their own damage while they help lead the recovery. Still rough out there, but each day we adapt to the new reality while we restore paradise. I am surrounded by very large and beautiful spirits. The bodies come in all sizes and abilities. Everyone does what they can. We got this. ❤️🖤

Happy GoLucky
October 7 at 5:07pm ·
Some dear friends graced us with a visit last night. It was a fun and healing evening. Bruised and battered, tired and sleepy people enjoying the pleasure and strength of friendship. Much laughter, many yawns, infinite love. ❤️🖤

Happy GoLucky

October 8 at 7:12am ·

Sunday! No personal siren screaming emergencies currently. I declare a Day of Rest for Happy GoLucky crew.

Happy GoLucky shared Charlotte Quinn's post.

October 8 at 9:30am ·

Charlotte Quinn

September 27 at 10:34am ·

I just want to thank Dion of All Keys Area Roofing. She is out there working hard to help all who need her. She doesn't care if you are rich or poor or friend or not. She has been there for everyone. Thank you a dion and Deb for what you are doing for our City

Happy GoLucky Really! 

October 8 at 6:41am

Happy GoLucky

October 8 at 10:07am ·

As the service industry struggles to recover we are there to support y'all. Take a break, go get an ice cream, a sandwich, or beer. Hell, go sit down for a full meal. You need it, they need it. Today's word is a step up from the usual Keys practice of over-tipping. For a bit, if you got it, please TIP STUPID BIG! You'll be glad you did.

Happy GoLucky

October 9 at 8:11am ·

Monday, 10/9/2017. Up very early to do my chores. After I woke up the sun, (one of my primary duties), I checked what y'all here on Facebook had to say. Life goes on, and there's only so long you can make crisis the perspective. Still, "normal" life has taken on a vastly different meaning here in the Florida Keys. Those of us who still have homes are trying to repair damages. Those without homes are scrambling to find housing. The lucky ones with no damage are trying to adjust to the major changes in the town, help neighbors and friends recover, and keep their spirits high. Here, at the Happy GoLucky abode, we will continue to haul yard & storm debris to the curb. We also need to catch up on whatever came in the mail lately. Body benefited from a day off yesterday. Feeling good, feeling strong. Later I will feel beat up and tired, but that's getting familiar and I can deal. Had a visit from sweet girls last night. We sat down to a nice meal and a wonderful pumpkin pie with ice cream. Love them girls. ❤🖤 All of us have much work to do. Life is full of challenge. Doesn't matter if you're young or old, rich or poor. You still got to carry that weight. Do it with love, do it with grace. You can ask for a helping hand, but don't put your burden on anybody Else's back. You're strong, know that you can do this. We love you. Together we all will restore this town to the paradise we love.

Happy GoLucky

October 10 at 5:30am ·

Tuesday, 10/10/2017. Another night with little sleep, but enough to last the day. That Lucky Old Sun is still sleeping in my part of the world. Yesterday, I talked about moving from a perspective of crisis into that of a "new normal". Today I realized that I had dated yesterday's post with September as the month. (Edited and corrected.) So much for getting a grip. So much for establishing "new normal." Saying it's ok doesn't make it ok. But we ARE making it ok. Each day brings a better understanding that things have changed in major ways. Each day brings more acceptance of our reality. It's now been one month since Irma kicked our asses.

No doubt about it, she came here with bad intent and left a mark. But the miracle is that WE"RE STILL STANDING (figuratively for me}. The people who cling to these rocks like barnacles won't be driven out by this event. LOVE & STRENGTH are here on awesome display. Neighbors, friends and total strangers are lifting each other out of this quagmire. Our public officials are managing to maintain order in the face of chaos. Our businesses are serving customers. Kids are in school. Life goes on. Each day it gets a little better in our community. What hurts is that each day we learn about good people who got hit so very hard. It's heartbreaking. But no one alive "lost everything." If you are breathing, then you have the most important commodity this life offers. You have a fighting chance to recover. Feel joy in that realization. Know that you still have resources. People are good. People will help. Stay Strong. I love you.

Happy GoLucky
October 10 at 9:18am ·
Long Shot: Anybody in Crane Hammock (or anywhere) find a 16' aluminum extension ladder? If so, give me a shout. It just might be the one that used to live here before the storm.

Happy GoLucky
October 10 at 6:02pm ·
Any of my friends need a good running Conch Cruiser for cheap? Evacuated by air, drove home in new car, At least one car too many now. No flooding on this (bay) side. Selling "as is", but has always been dependable. Good tires, battery, brakes, etc. Not a looker, but no rust or rot. Holler if you're interested.

Happy GoLucky
October 11 at 6:18am ·
Wednesday, 10/11/2017. "Hump Day" for all of you who work a Monday to Friday job. Here in the Keys, many people work in the service industry and few get the weekend off. Folks call their last

day of work before their day(s) off "My Friday." Since the storm, every day is Monday. Every day is Ground Hog Day. Tune up; Start to Play; Just like every other day. The days blur, the dates are relevant only because bills have due dates. Yet, each day is a new day. Each day is a new chance to do something good and useful. Each day we recommit our determination to rebuild our community. Each day we strengthen the bonds that join us together. Yesterday was mixed. One of the Happy GoLucky crew was sidelined by cumulative wear & tear. Physical labor in tropical conditions takes its toll. Nothing major, nothing rest won't cure. ML & I did a little in the yard, took care of some business, and got tree bracing materials and other needs from Home Depot. My exhausted roofer neighbors called late last night when they got home. They are troopers who work long days trying to help people put their homes back together. The estimate for my roof will wait until today. The tarps on my roof are keeping us dry so far. The contract haulers cleared the refuse pile we hauled to the street. I noticed that one of the huge temporary dumps on the highway had been reduced by half. Its still gimongous. The volunteers from the nearby church may help us raise some trees and help with cutting up the trees that are beyond saving. All-in-all, a good day. Today looms. Folks are tired. Folks are strong. Coffee is more than a beverage, it's a miracle drug. My dose just arrived. Time to caffeine up and start the war chants. Keep letting us feel your love, it helps more than I can say. I Love you. 🩷
🖤

Happy GoLucky
October 11 at 5:27pm ·

Emily H., ML and I were making good progress in the yard. Then we were joined by Saint Columba volunteers Michael, James and Diane. They were STELLAR!! We got so much done today! Really starting to look OK! So Happy, So Grateful. 🩷🖤

Happy GoLucky

October 12 at 2:08am ·

Thursday, 10/12/2017. It's 1:05 a.m. Have slept in fits and starts since crashing shortly after supper. Now I'm wide awake. The body wants a massage, but that's not gonna happen. Heat and hard work cramp muscles. It's hard to drink enough to stay properly hydrated. This recovery work is no joke. But yesterday's accomplishments are balm to sore muscles. Had an enormous lift in the recovery of the yard from Diane, James and Michael who are doing volunteer work organized by Saint Columba Church. Reverend Debra has been in the forefront of community work since her arrival some years ago. Her visibility in the Irma recovery is remarkable. I encourage everyone with a need to reach out to Saint Columba. They have supplies and volunteers that might meet your need. Lord knows they will try to help you. We were able to raise many of the fallen trees. Those beyond saving got cut up and hauled to the curb. Dead branches caught in trees were removed. Broken limbs were trimmed with fresh cuts. The raised trees are held in place by ratchet straps and ropes temporarily. We need to go back and secure these trees with wooden tripod bracing before removing the temporary rigging. Big job, but nothing we can't handle. The hammock has been thinned drastically, but it survives and is starting to heal. I hope the rains hold until everyone (and me) has a roof, but rain is what the hammock needs now. Rain will bring new life to the trees that remain. I can't wait to see everything turn green again. This unique semi-tropical high hardwood hammock is a magical place. We love it so and feel blessed to live here. We love that our neighbors share that sentiment. Started paying bills very early yesterday morning. Not a fun way to begin the day, but nice to know we are taking care of business. Things have been such a blur, it's easy to miss meeting due dates. Think we're caught up for the moment. Funny how disaster can create an inverse relationship between income and expenses. So many folks have lost their jobs because the businesses which employed them are closed. Yet, they are faced with the extraordinary costs of recovery. This isn't going to get solved overnight, but time is the great healer. Now that it's fairly safe to walk through the yard, our attention will shift to the house. There's much to do, but we have a livable situation. Roof (no estimate yet), siding, soffit, fascia, screens, porch ceiling fans . . . so much to do. It will take time, patience, money and hard work - and a little luck. Well, I've said my piece. Now I'm going to see if any of y'all have updated FB with what you've been doing, what help you need. Gonna check all the usual public info spots as well. Then it will be time to wake up the sun, drink coffee and start the war chants in preparation of today's battle. Stay strong! I love you.

Happy GoLucky
October 12 at 6:42am ·
YouTube
Preparing for Battle

Cheyenne War Dance

This is a traditional Northern Cheyenne war dance. When I heard it I thought "I MUST make a video about this". If anyone who watches my video who is a Cheyene

Happy GoLucky More strong, black coffee please!

The Gift of Tragedy

Happy GoLucky shared CBS Miami's post.
Yesterday at 12:04am ·
CBS Miami
October 12 at 8:15pm ·
#EXCLUSIVE: Under an emergency contract awarded through the Florida Department of Transportation, issued by Florida Gov. Rick Scott, two companies are being paid anywhere from three to 10 times more to do the same work that another was doing under a separate agreement the firm has with Monroe County.

(Report by Jim DeFede)

Exclusive: Debris Debacle In Keys After Gov. Scott Issues Emergency DOT Contract

It is believed that the debris removal rates for these emergency contracts are the highest being paid for anywhere in the state of Florida.

Happy GoLucky

Friday, 10/13/2017.
It rained yesterday. The rain was soft and there wasn't any wind. Haven't noticed any leaks from the tarped roof. Hope that continues. Spent the day making calls and connections, looking up needed information, planning and keeping my swollen feet elevated. TMI? If so, sorry - but that's the way it is here. My body rarely gets to do what it wants. But it does a decent job of doing what it must. Thank you, body. I'd promise you I won't abuse you anymore, but I can't manage to say that with a straight face. As usual, crashed immediately after supper. Woke up at the beginning of the 2nd quarter of Thursday Night Football. Just in time to see Cam Newton walk into the end zone to put the PANTHERS up 10 to 3 over my EAGLES. Damn, should have slept a little longer. The Birds fought back, and we left Carolina with a road win over a very good team. Could it be that this EAGLES team is for real? Fell back to sleep watching the late shows. That sleep didn't last too long. At some point in the night, heard violent animal noises. I think a night hawk might have gotten the better of a squirrel. Thankfully, it was a brief battle. Survival of the fittest is more than a saying. On the Happy News front, my friend Harry dropped off a pair of really cool magnifying glasses. You know, what us old folk call cheaters. I've got dozens of broken dollar store cheaters scattered about the house. What's cool about these "Clic" glasses is that they're already broken. They hang around your neck and there are strong magnets that join the two halves at the nose. Sounds weird, but works like a charm. Easy Peasy. I take great pleasure in little things. Well, time to fuel up on coffee, wake up the sun and start the war chants. Gotta win the battle before you can win the war. Stay Strong. I love you. 🩷🖤

Happy GoLucky

Fueled up, weather clear, ready for take-off. Wait, I better put on pants. 😎😎

The Gift of Tragedy

Happy GoLucky

Saturday, 10/14/2017. 2:00 a,m,

Been up for an hour just trying to sort reality. Funny thing, reality. It seems to change drastically and constantly. Could it be that life is dynamic? My dear friend, Todd M. D., lost his mother early yesterday, He and Renee J. are in my heart. I feel their loss. My mother passed in June. The go-get-em attitude produced by coffee and war chants turned into a quieter reflection on loss and mortality. Later in the day; got downstairs and tried to log an accomplishment. Emily H. took down the remainder of the hanging fiberglass insulation from the 13ft. high floor joists of our elevated house. We've been unwrapping this mess since our return on 9/21. The stuff hanging under the house was the last of Irma's attempt to decorate our house, yard and cars for Halloween. Still bits and pieces here and there, but mostly bagged and gone. Good riddance! OK, then the texts started coming from Sprint. Seems that autopay didn't autoswitch when we were issued a new credit card number after some merchant got hacked. Tried following instructions. Dialed *2 and hit a wall. When did it first become clear that the machines that manage us don't like customers talking to real people? Many curses later I broke through menu hell and got some customer service guy seemingly based offshore. Problem quickly resolved by human. He didn't ask me to press or say any numbers. Town had several entertainment options last night. Bars and restaurants are hosting parties to celebrate advances in recovery. Went to a friends for a minute to bs and drink a beer. Nicest part of the day. Came home, made and ate a meatball sub. Crashed hard. Now, I'm up and talking to you. I'll gather the news of the day, check what y'all wrote about your reality. That information will affect my thinking, give me ideas and insights as to my priorities. Then it will be time to wake the sun. Sun don't care about all this. Sun just wants to shine and roll around heaven all day. Me, I'm counting the minutes until coffee. Then the war chants and a return to the battle. The easy decisions are mostly made. The more difficult ones pile up; The trick is to do the next thing. Put a pin in the rest. Those things ain't going anywhere. They will be there when their turn comes. Onward and Upward. Stay Strong. I love you. 🩷🖤

Happy GoLucky

Sunday, 10/15/2017. 12:53 a.m.

Yesterday felt good. Body was feeling ok after a morning of dilly-dallying, much coffee, and listening to war chants. I was up and at 'em by crack of 1:00 p.m. Mary Lou, Emily and I worked on a variety of things, nothing monumental - but worthy tasks. Starting to be able to find things again. We enjoyed the work. Anytime you can be in the moment and enjoying your life is a gift. Knocked off reasonably early and I knocked back a couple cold ones. Em & I shared recollections of times past here in the Keys. Wild, fun times. We smiled at the memories of dear friends passed. They live in the stories we tell. ML made a delicious supper which I ate with gusto. After supper, went down hard. Woke just before 11:00 p.m. Been up   since.

Should get the skinny on the roof on Monday. Today, not really a football Sunday. My Eagles played on Thursday. Sunday is my day of rest regardless. I only do emergency work on this day. I don't consider helping friends work, I call that recreation. So, I may do some of that. If not, might take a ride to Key West. Kinda not wanting to see the lower keys between Marathon & KW. I hear it's as bad in some places as the photos indicate. Even those places will recover. Key West is always fun. Really could use more sleep. I'm going to give it a shot. Will add more later.

Sunday, 3:37 a.m. - Got back to sleep for a few. Shoulder cramps said it was time to wake up. Groggy but waking fast. Feels good to sit up and shrug, do neck rolls. Fingers like typing. Getting old is still a lot better than the alternative. It's a long time before I need to wake the sun. Much too long until the coffee pours. Might take one more shot at sleep in a bit. One of the small but satisfying tasks accomplished yesterday was to relieve a borrowed "come along" winch from duty. It had been holding tension on a raised tree-keeping it upright. Freed up a ratchet strap from wind tie-down duty and used it as a replacement for the come along. What is satisfying is that I can return the come along to the lender, my good neighbor Matt. I hate to borrow tools. The third time I borrow a tool is when I decide I need to buy one of my own. I have a reverence for tools. Used them all my life from a little kid until now. I always try to return a borrowed tool in better condition than it was before I used it. Matt takes care of his tools. The come along was in good condition. Still, I wiped it down and oiled everything, played out the wire rope to remove kinks. Respect. Gonna give sleep one more shot.

Sunday, 6:00 a.m. - Woke slowly and carefully. All my body parts passed the check. Noted that sun still has an hour and 22 minutes to sleep. Not sure when the coffee will be ready. ML has warned me that she needs her sleep. The price of coffee in bed is that you can't make it yourself. That's actually a good thing. I'd be drinking coffee at midnight and never get any sleep at all. Today will be special, just like every other day, only better. Katy and Louise taught me that it will be the Best Day Ever! So going to enjoy this perfect day. No war chants today. But there will be a wonderful breakfast. 😋 😊 Stay Strong. I love you. ❤️🖤

Happy GoLucky

Sun's up; coffee beans in the grinder; got a Good Morning kiss from the most beautiful woman in the world. Life is very, very good. 😎 

Happy GoLucky

Should be fun. Thanks to all who make this possible. Suggest that you bring an umbrella, big hat, some way to keep that noon to six sun from melting you.

Happy GoLucky

Monday, 10/16/2017. 2:48 a.m. And I've been up for a couple hours. I see that too many of my friends are awake also. Don't you people ever sleep? :) Sorry, not funny. I know that you wish you were sound asleep. I know I wish I was. Had a nice breakfast yesterday. As I've stated in previous posts, the Eagles played Thursday, so I was footloose and fancy free on this football Sunday. Decided to take the new car to Key West. Funny thing about the new car. Bought it in North Carolina for the return from Irma evacuation. Drove home in a daze of exhaustion. Parked the car. Yesterday is the first time I drove it since our return on 9/21. Pretty nice car! Thank you, Charles Dabney. Made the day trip a pleasure. First car we've owned that was made in this century. The technology sure has changed. This car has so many bells and whistles that the driver is just another passenger. Set the cruise and it follows the car in front of you. It slows when they slow. It stops when they stop. It tells you if you leave your lane, It warns you when someone is in your blind spot. It tells you when to turn, It answers phone calls and text. It will read a text to you. There was a time when I would have hated the machine telling me what to do. I've surrendered. The war between man and machine is over. They won. Just sit back and enjoy the sound system.

The drive down to Key West from Marathon got mixed reviews as

to the condition of the lower Keys. I was impressed by how much had survived. ML thought the damage was pretty bad. I'm thinking we are both accurate in our assessments. ML & I had supper in KW with Bz Z. and Amy J. who operate THE SALTY ANGLER on Duval Street. We dined outdoors at ONLYWOOD, a collective favorite. It was nice to spend time with good friends and pull them away from work for a minute. After supper, Bz and I stopped by another of the many fine KW establishments. Don't remember the name of the place, but it had a good vibe. When the bartender learned I was from Marathon, she told me that she was headed there in the morning with 7 trucks loaded with cleaning and building supplies. There's lots of free recovery items available. There are lots of people in need. The difficulty has been in matching need with stuff. "Laurie" took my number and a few suggestions of folks that might be able to help her get her stuff to those in need. I will do all in my power to get the stuff to those who can use it. All help; all suggestions greatly appreciated. I should know more specifics about what she's bringing in a few hours. She mentioned tarps, 1"x3"s; rakes, shovels, cleaning supplies. Don't know what else. Somebody needs this stuff. Let's try to get it to them. My wonderful neighbors are coming for supper this evening. They were stellar in keeping an eye on our house while we were away. They got our roof tarped immediately after the storm. Time to discuss a new roof. Dion Watson of All Area Roofing and Waterproofing put a new metal roof on the house next door last year. It's ground floor, so I had a bird's eye view of the work from my elevated house. Quality work quickly done. Dion's crew left the work site clean, a sign of professionalism. That roof went through Irma without any damage. The owner of that roof is very pleased. One of the requirements of obtaining a roofing license is that the person seeking a license must be of good moral character. Good requirement! You don't want to be sitting under a roof by done by a fly-by-night roofer.

 ;)

Gonna wrap this and check on what my friends, the community and the world are doing. As always, I'll wake the sun, drink copious amounts of black coffee, start the war chants and join the battle. Stay Strong. I love you, ♥🖤

Happy GoLucky

Went to Key West for some R&R today. Met a gal who says she's got 7 pickup loads of building and cleaning supplies she's bringing to Marathon tomorrow. Her name is Laurie and she's got these supplies stored at MM9. She's clearing that space out and shutting it down. Her outfit is called KeysStrong. She's looking for folks in need who want this stuff. I suggested the American Legion and Saint Columba. Not sure if either organization is still accepting donations. Push comes to shove, I'll take what I can fit and you can come here to pick it up. If you're hard pressed for transportation, maybe we can get stuff delivered. As I learn more about what's available, I'll let you know, In the meantime, tell me who might distribute these supplies. Let me know who needs what. Stay Strong. I love you. ♥🖤

Happy GoLucky

Okay, so Laurie, Stacy and Steve from KeysStrong came up here with a truckload of stuff. If you need rakes, shovels, charcoal, a charcoal grill, bleach, mops, buckets, sponges, personal toiletries, more, I can hook you up. Post here or send me a P.M. We deliver. FREE. Please Share.

<u>Happy GoLucky</u>
"Why don't you move"? A picture is worth 10,000 words.

<u>Happy GoLucky</u>
Good morning, Babies! Yes, I wake up the sun. You're welcome.  ♥😎😎

<u>Happy GoLucky</u>
Tuesday, 10/17/2017.
It's four o'clock in the morning. Somewhere nearby a man is screaming "You don't have to go home, but you can't stay here." Life is pretty much same as it always was. A person, a town, a country, can only live in a state of emergency so long before that emergency state becomes normalized. People adapt quickly. Life is dynamic. Folks grow old, other folks grow up. Births, deaths, weddings and funerals. The wheel keeps turning. Our town got whacked hard by Hurricane Irma. Lives were turned upside down. But in the midst of this tragedy, you saw the resiliency of the human spirit. You saw folks rise to the occasion. The thing about catastrophe is that you can't sleep walk through your normal routine. The snow globe of your life gets shaken, and everything falls into place in a new way. But it settles and life goes on. The picture is recognizable. Routines become reestablished. The gift of tragedy is that it reminds you of

the important things. Don't forget how you feel. Take that reminder into the future and let the love for life, family, friends and fellow human beings grow. Sustain your desire to care for your brothers and sisters. Let your love light shine. Stay Strong. I love you. 🩷🖤

Happy GoLucky

Wednesday, 10/18/2017.

It's hump day for those of you who work Monday to Friday. It's another Keep Humping day for Florida Keys Recovery. Still so much to do. But there's a massive amount that has been done. I'm thinking that Christmas is a reasonable goal for our town to exhale. No, we won't have everything done by then. It may take years to eradicate all the damage wrought by Hurricane Irma. But Santa shouldn't have any trouble getting his sleigh around our town. The Happy-Go-Lucky crew pressure washed stairs and vinyl siding on the elevator shaft yesterday. Mary Lou and Emily did a fantastic job. I managed to do enough to get soaking wet. No biggie, the Goldilocks weather kept me comfortable. Emily H. and I have distributed the bulk of the supplies from Laurie at KeysStrong. We still have a bunch of rakes and some other stuff you might find useful. Post to my page or drop us a P.M. if you have a need. We just might have what you want. As usual, up and down most of the night. I still see way too many folks I know wandering around Facebook in the wee hours of the new day. Insomnia is the new craze. I haven't slept in consecutive hours for many years, so nothing new here. But I'm concerned that so many others are developing interrupted sleep patterns. Y'all just aren't trained in functioning under these conditions. I count on many of you to run the world. Get some rest. 🥴😵‍💫 Getting close to time to wake the sun. Coffee renews the energy and courage of sore muscles. The war summon the spirit to battle. The war continues. We are happy warriors. Stay Strong. I Love You. 🩷🖤

The Gift of Tragedy

Happy GoLucky

Irma hit the Florida Keys beginning on 9/9/2017 and stayed here way too long. We got whacked big time. Since then, there have been far too many other catastrophic events that have affected too many lives. We send love to the folks in Puerto Rico, Las Vegas, Northern California and elsewhere. We know you are hurting too. The news shifts to the latest tragic event. The nation suffers from short attention span syndrome. Our personal lives must take precedence over all else. But please keep sending love to the folks clinging to these rocks in the Southernmost part of our nation. Feeling your love helps us stay strong. It means more to us than I could ever explain. Thank you from the bottom of my heart. I love you. ❤🖤

Happy GoLucky

Thursday, 10/19/2017.

It's 5:32 a.m. Soon the good folks of Marathon Garbage Service will come by to haul our "recyclables" away. There's something surreal about the return of scheduled collection of our ordinary household waste being classified as trash, which is picked up on Mondays and Fridays; Gardening debris arranged neatly and picked up on Tuesday; and Recyclables which get hauled away on Thursdays.

Meanwhile, I was at the Middle School/High School yesterday to give the neighbor girls a ride home and saw MOUNTAINS of every kind of refuse piled ENORMOUSLY HIGH within feet of the schools. Strange days indeed. It reminds me of living in the center of Philadelphia. You could see unimaginable wealth and splendor on one block, Turn the corner and things might be very, very different. One had to know their way around.

40

The Gift of Tragedy

The opportunity to fill in for "Mom's Taxi" was a treat. ML, the girls and I stopped at the Island Diner for ice cream (I had a burger.) You can use kids as an excuse to do stuff like eat ice cream, go to Disneyland, ride amusements, etc. I knew there had to be a reason so many people agree to serve these MiniMe's for 18 years. It's nice when you can borrow a couple kids and indulge in a mid-afternoon treat. That, and these girls are delightful company.
Just like the duality of "normal" waste collection contrasted by mountains of storm waste being hauled by disaster contractors, our lives have that same dissonance in many ways. Things are different living under a blue tarp. But in many ways, they are still the same. Eat, sleep (sort of), brush your teeth, pay your bills . . . all while you hear chainsaws and Bobcats hard at work. At the end of the day ML & I took a walk around the neighborhood, this was the first time I've done this since the storm. The landscape has changed, A large number of trees were lost. Many of them still need to be cut and hauled away. There are piles of vegetative debris everywhere. This was surprising, since our block is mostly clear. Our dear friend who lives across the street joined us mid-walk. We went down to the Gulf of Mexico. The scene was like a beautiful still life painting. The water was placid, the clouds didn't move. It was very quiet. There were flocks of Great Blue Herons in unusually large numbers. We saw flocks of egrets and large flocks of other birds that we couldn't identify. This was easily the most birds I ever saw in flight at this spot. The totality of the water, clouds, and the birds illuminated by the setting sun was . . . special. Life is good.
Stay Strong. I Love You. 🩷🖤

Happy GoLucky shared Derrick Johnson post.
And Pow! Just got the call from Home Depot on the delivery. The order got bigger.

910 sheets of 1/2" drywall
13 boxes (25lbs ea) of 1 1/4" drywall screws
3 boxes (25lbs ea) of 2" drywall screws

3 boxes (25lbs ea) of 2 1/2" drywall screws
100 rolls of drywall tape (500' each)
96 pails of drywall compound
556 rolls of R13 Insulation

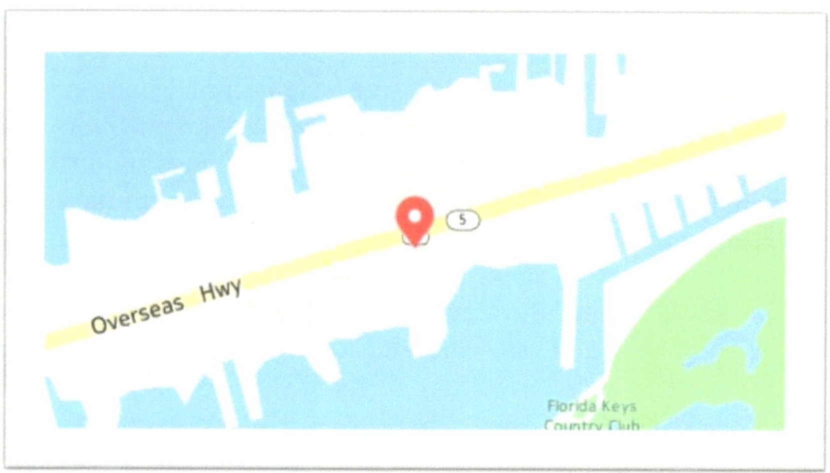

<u>American Legion Post 154, Marathon, Florida</u>
Armed Forces · Marathon, FL

Happy GoLucky Been flooded? Had to tear out your drywall? P.M Derrick with your name, address, phone number and how many sheets of drywall you would like to pick-up. Just spoke with him. He's expecting delivery soon.

Happy GoLucky
Friday, 10/20/2017.
Not much to say. Plenty to do. Rested battered body and spent the rainy day trying to help folks with problems find help. Also spent too much time voicing my opinions on a number of subjects. This confirms that my days on Facebook are limited. I'm not a person who can remain silent and keep my opinion to myself when I see an issue I want to address. But you know the deal on opinions, they're like elbows - most people have a couple. And like your elbows, they

aren't much use to the other folk. The adrenaline summoned by the initial dig-out is less available as we move from emergency to long term recovery. The challenge will be to sustain our desire to help others as we deal with our personal challenges. The old saying that charity begins at home isn't quite accurate. Charity begins in your loving heart. Keep your love alive. Ask for the help you need. Give the help you can. I love you. Stay Strong.

(P.S.) I'll be here for a while more. It's important to communicate in this way while we work to recover our paradise. I promise not to disappear without notice as I did three years ago. But my time here talking to virtual friends isn't without an expiration date. You know how to find me in real life.

Happy GoLucky

Don't know anything about the Crisis Relief Team, but I can vouch for the accuracy of what is captured in this video. We have work to do; today, tomorrow and for some time to come. There's a party in the Marathon City Park tomorrow. Put down your burdens for a bit, come out and laugh and play with your friends and neighbors. We're in this for the long haul. Pace yourself. Lean on me. I'm sure as hell gonna lean on you. We got this. Stay Strong. I love you.

Happy GoLucky

Saturday, 10/21/2017.

The sun is shining at the moment. There's a party in the park that starts at noon. Bring an umbrella for rain or sun, or at least a hat with a brim. Folding chairs are also a good idea. Free food and music and laughter. Enjoy the day and refresh your spirit. Rest those tired muscles. Planning to eat sushi at Takara with loved friends after the party. Looking forward to seeing them. We've all been way too busy. Passed ML's beloved 1999 Subaru sedan to a new owner yesterday. Think it will serve our good friend well. Shocking how few miles it has been driven. Oldie but a goodie. I like to turn wrenches - to a point. ML inherits my 1999 Honda CR-V for running around town. We now have a vehicle made in this century for longer trips. Back to pressure washing on Monday. On break today and tomorrow. Still got free rakes and a few other things if you need 'em. P.M. me. Well, try your best to rest. If you can't, be careful and Stay Strong. I love you. ❤️🖤

Happy GoLucky

Random thought: Facebook is constantly reminding me of things I posted in previous years. I'd like to remind everyone of a memory of not-so-long-ago. Remember how lucky and grateful you felt to be alive the day after Irma passed? Has that gratitude subsided? Keep it strong, it's the silver lining behind the storm clouds. Don't squander your gift. ❤️🖤

Happy GoLucky shared John Bartus's post.

Post Irma-Geddon Feel-Good Saturday (this Saturday) lineup:

12:00 - Dan Sullivan
12:45 - Ty Thurman
1:30 - John Bartus
2:15 - Freddie Bye
3:15 - Joe Mama
4:00 - In Pursuit
5:00 - Jade Storm

Also, Randy Barnett (Fiddle Rock) will be jamming along with whomever... Free burgers, dogs, water, kid's games... and bring your own coolers and lawn chairs! Here's more info in this video courtesy of Marathon TV88:

Join John Bartus & Local Musicians at the Post Irma-Geddon Feel-Good Saturday from 12pm-6pm at Marathon Community Park in Marathon, Florida Keys October 21.

Happy GoLucky
YOU DESERVE A BREAK TODAY! 

Happy GoLucky
Sunday, 10/22/2017.
Spent the morning talking to roofers about next steps. Made some headway. There are some unresolved structural issues. We all want to get it right. Dion and Deb are easy to work with and take pride in doing a good job. We will get this lined out. Got out relatively early Saturday to check out the giveaway at D'Asign Source, a local contractor with a showroom offering a wide variety of products. Well attended, well organized and very generous event. Lots of cool stuff went home with happy people. I took home an electrical main breaker box and ML got a gallon of Kilz primer to cover the minor rain water stains on the ceiling were the roof leaked before it got tarped. Thanks D'Asign Source! Nice party at City Park yesterday. Good burgers cooked by and compliments of the Rotary. Great local music. I like to stay positive, but it would be less than honest if I didn't say that smoke from the nearby "vegetative" burn detracted from the festivities. Still, the vibe was good, the crowd appreciative and determined to have a good time.
Went out to a favorite Thia restaurant later and met good friends for supper. Food was outstanding, the company superb. Learned that one of our friends is a "creature of culture." It's good to laugh, and laugh we did.
Glad that my Eagles play in the Sunday Night game. Means the game against the Washington Politically Incorrect Team Name will be nationally televised. I don't have to go to a Sunday Ticket bar. Nice to get horizontal while I view. LET"S GO EAGLES!!! Been nice mostly kicking back yesterday and today. Too much work and no play make's folks dull. I don't wanna be a star, I just want to shine.
The war is waiting in the wings. Battle stations in the morning. Stay Strong. I Love You.

Happy GoLucky
Monday, 10/23/2017

Life continues to run on two tracks. Marathon Garbage Service dutifully hauled away the little bit of household trash we've produced since the Friday collection. I'll go back to paying my bills on Monday mornings. I'll watch my Philadelphia Eagles on cable television from the comfort of my home tonight. I also have my choice of cool bars where I could watch the game, eat good food, drink my choice of beverages. There's great live music if that's what I'm wanting. If I go outside I'll see my torn screens flapping in the breeze. I'll hear chainsaws and machinery engaged in restoring paradise. I can look up at my roof and see that it's covered in blue plastic. I can see the missing siding, soffit and fascia. I can see the blown down trees. I know there are mountains of storm debris still to be cleared. It's so different. It's so the same. At least for me. I so recognize that some folks are still in the emergency status where they are scrambling to find stability, shelter, work . . . safety. EVERYBODY wants to help. We do what we can, but there are no magic wands that will restore everybody to their previous status and take away their troubles. All we can do is all we can do, and we're doing it every day in every way. Coffee in my belly, music on the box. Ready for today, the Best Day Ever! I love you. Stay Strong. 

Happy GoLucky
It's Tuesday, 10/24/2017.

The big issue here in Marathon seems to be the decision of the City to get rid of the debris at the Golf Course classified as "Vegetative" by setting it on fire. We were told in advance of the burning that it wouldn't cause any problems. That hasn't quite been how the burning is playing out. I'm lucky to be mostly upwind, and if I wasn't I'd get upwind. My breathing smoke at City Park on Saturday was quite enough, thank you. The thing that concerns me most is the division it's causing between those who see the burning as a serious health risk and those who want them to stop complaining. As I said,

The Gift of Tragedy

I'm not breathing the smoke, so I don't have a strong opinion other than that folks experiencing health problems need to stop breathing that smoke. As an evacuee, I understand the difficulties of even a short relocation. Honest I do. But your first duty is to protect your health. If you want to fight the burning, do so after you get out of that smoke. The recovery continues. The cacophony of chain saws, Bobcats, end-loaders, dump trucks, and other instruments of this grand symphony still fills the air. Folks are still getting flats on a regular basis from nails and screws that bite tires. But the latest beach report says the water's fine. The sunsets are still beautiful. Offshore, the fishing is good. I can still sit outside in a tee shirt night or day. Since the privacy provided by trees is mostly gone I'm wearing pants, so that's a change Irma imposed. I'm still living in Paradise and I can't think of anywhere else I'd rather be. FEMA has an office in town now. I might go up and say Hi, but they haven't shown much inclination to help me. Guy came and took five phone pics soon after our return. Said that because we were living in our house we shouldn't expect any assistance. He also said he was just the advance man; that the "real guy" (his words) would visit us and make a determination. Next day we got a refusal letter and haven't heard anything since. FEMA did put us up in a hotel one night in Jacksonville as we made our way home from North Carolina. So I can't say they haven't done anything for us. 😊;)
Want to give a shout out to the many organization and individuals helping folks in need. Y'all stepping up big time and doing heroic and saintly work. I won't name names for fear of leaving someone out, but I want you to know you're my heroes! ♥🖤
OK, on to the best thing that happened yesterday. MONDAY NIGHT FOOTBALL! FLY, EAGLES, FLY! 6-1 Baby!!! Starting to become a believer. Maybe, just maybe. It's early, so caution remains.
"Your favorite band" the Red Elvises are in town at the newly reopened Key Colony Inn tonight. Guaranteed to be Fun! City Council is also meeting tonight. Guaranteed to be entertaining! Timing allows you to attend both events. Keep your heads up, love your neighbors. Stay Strong. We got this! I Love you. ♥🖤

The Gift of Tragedy

Happy GoLucky

Frisky little thunderstorm going on at 3:20. a.m. Hang tough, blue tarp! 😜 ;)

Happy GoLucky

Wednesday, 10/25/2017.

Another day in Paradise. Kinda rainy, but not too much wind. Weather girl (weather woman? weather person?) on my tv says it's gonna dry out for the next couple days. Good, that big campfire at the Golf Course doesn't need any more challenges. Despite the raging Facebook controversy over the smoke, not a single person voiced a concern at last night's City Council meeting. Burn on!

With all the excitement of the recovery it slipped my mind that Fantasy Fest is happening down in Key West. Pretty fun event. Kinda like Mardi Gras, but sexier. Don't bring your kids to Duval if you don't want them to see some nudity. (Don't take them to the library if you don't want them to see books.) I'm thinking maybe take a ride down on Friday and celebrate the weirdness. The parade is cool on Saturday. If you've never been, put this on your bucket list. If you're going, stop by The Salty Angler on Duval Street and say Hi to my friends Amy & Bz. Lots to do here. Cleanup continues. You're tired of hearing about it; I'm tired of talking about it. Just keep us in your hearts. Coffee-ing up, switched from war chants to funk. Pump, pump, pump it up! Keep dancing. Keep smiling. Keep love alive. Ask for the help you need. Give the help you can. Stay Strong. I love you. ❤️🖤

Get Up Offa That Thing 1976

The Gift of Tragedy

Happy GoLucky

Thursday, 10/26/2017.

Plunged down to 68°f last night. Winter is here! Thankfully, this frigid weather is only a two-day event and the days are warmer than the nights.

The City of Marathon has received permission from the Forestry Service to burn the vegetative debris 24/7. Previously, the fire could only burn from dawn until dusk. It should burn hotter now and produce less smoke. We shall see. One thing seems certain, the vegetative debris will be gone at an earlier date.

Sun is shining bright. I'm half full on the caffeine meter, coffee cup in hand. Might venture down to Key West and the Green Parrot to hear the 5:30 sound check for the Red Elvises. Fun band with killer musicians. Nice people too. If you never heard them, you owe it to yourself to catch them sometime. They tour 8 days a week, so they're bound to be in your town before long.

Fantasy Fest is in full swing. The die-hard Marathon Krewe says they're gonna show in the parade. The float's a little rough as of yesterday. Seems impossible to pull together that quick. In this town we accomplish the impossible every day, usually before lunch. Safe bet I'll be waving at them as they parade by on Saturday night and the float will be outstanding. Big ups to Neil Cataldo & Krewe.

Folks are slowly coming out of shock and starting to understand the new reality here. They are figuring out just what they need to go forward. There's a lot of stuff available that you might need. Ask.

Someone probably has it or knows where you can get it.

Singer Jen is playing the 'Cane tonight 7-10. Free admission. She's fantastic. Irrepressible smile, awesome music. Go see her, and leave something in her tip jar if you can.

That's the news from my rock for now. We keep on keeping on. We get by with a little help from our friends. Thank you for being a friend, it means the world to me. If you read this, please click something to let me know you stopped by. Things get better each and every day. Keep the love flowing. Stay Strong. I love you. 🩷🖤

Happy GoLucky
Friday, 10/27/2017.
Went to Key West last night. Had a blast! Saw the RED ELVISES' 5:30 show at the GREEN PARROT. The Elvises are a cool blend of expert musicianship, comedy theater and Rok N Roll. As usual, they got the room, the bellies and the asses shaking. Bz Z. and Amy J. were waiting for us outside after the set. We all had drinks and a bite at MARY ELLEN'S, a relatively new bar in the building that used to house the dance club WAX back in the day. Sorry to learn that a favorite bar and restaurant on the same street was closed because of Irma damage. TWO CENTS had a massive tree fall on it. Not sure when it will reopen, but I hope it's soon. Great place!
Later, ML and I strolled DUVAL STREET for a bit. Saw a number of friends and lots of other happy folks enjoying FANTASY FEST. I'm always impressed by how cut some bodies are, and how comfortable people shaped more like me are in walking the streets displaying their nudity. I don't even look in the mirror before I'm fully dressed. 😊 ;)
We continued our Promenade North on Duval until we reached Front Street. Crossed to the East side of the street and headed back South to THE SALTY ANGLER. HAPPY DOG was playing with all band members present. Damn, they are good! Hung with Amy Jones until we had to go. Love that girl! Headed back down Duval to pick up the auto parked just off Southard & Whitehead. The Elvises were in full swing playing their last set of the evening. We sat on the bench across the street and listened to them drive the crowd wild. Then it was time to call it a night. Got home in time to wake the sun and still get some rest before coffee. Absolutely a good time.
Gonna ease into today and let it take me where it will. No worries about not having stuff to do, something always jumps up and demands attention. But all work and no play make's you bored and boring. I'm a lot of things, but neither of those.

Yes, the lower Keys are still a mess between Marathon and Key West. Nonstop hauling hasn't changed the landscape of debris mountains noticeably. But the houses and boats aren't sitting in the middle of U.S.1 any longer. The recovery continues. It gets better every day. It will continue for quite a while. Take some time off. Devote a day or two to fun, leave your worries home and head to KW and enjoy the massive Fest party. You'll have a good time and be refreshed when you get home. Stay Strong. I love you. ❤️🖤

Happy GoLucky
Saturday, 10/28/2017.
What I want to be thinking about is watching the Fantasy Fest Parade tonight. What I'm thinking about is the weather in the Gulf of Mexico. Today is predicted to get very wet and real breezy. Hoping this weather doesn't get a name. Not really eager to check the integrity of the blue plastic roof I'm living under. There's still vinyl siding, soffit and fascia flapping around. I don't want to lose any more. But the weather will do what the weather does. We'll deal with it.
May be getting some reinforcements to help me with a few things. Gave a howl to the north; couple my Dawgs barked back. I see an airport pickup in my near future. True brothers.
I see how hard folks work just to get through the day. Sick kids, sick cars - late for work at their second job. But they get up each day and do it again. People are the best! Maybe someday we can stop arguing over bullshit and realize that most of us want the same things from life. It would be a whole lot easier if there wasn't so much profit in keeping us divided. I see the kindness, love and charity in folks that hate my politics and it makes me wish we could trade perspectives for a day instead of labels and stereotypes. Let's burn the straw man arguments and warm our hearts in that fire.
Time for more coffee. Keep love alive. Enjoy this Best Day Ever. Stay Strong. I love you. ❤️🖤

Happy GoLucky
Sunday, 10/29/2017.
After equivocating much of the day on Saturday, headed for Key West at 7:00 p.m. Hooked up with Bz Z. and Amy J. to watch the Fantasy Fest parade in front of THE SALTY ANGLER. Big fun. Floats were fantastic, the company even better. Sorry, Irma, you didn't rain on our parade. Neither did Tropical Depression 18. Turns out that I still like Havana Club rum.
Then it was Sunday. Got home in time to take a shower and still get to MARATHON GRILLE and ALE HOUSE to see 3 quarters of the Eagles V. 49ers. 7/1, baby! Monday, Monday will be here soon. Back to waking the sun and rolling the rock uphill. Marathon Rocks! Stay Strong, I love you. 🧡🖤

Happy GoLucky
Monday, 10/30/2017.
Monday morning, I pay my bills, so if I owe you money, check is in the mail. 😊;) Actually, I make a point of not being in debt. Not always the smartest way to do business, but it suits my personality. I'd rather do without than have to worry about paying bills for stuff I can't afford. I like being able to say what's on my mind without worrying that I might piss off the wrong person. I don't go out of my way to piss off anyone, but I don't worry when I do unless I've been thoughtless or unkind. When that happens (and it occasionally does) I try to learn from my mistakes and convert them into learning experiences. I'm being honest when I tell you that my one goal in life is to become a better man.
Things are still a mini-mess here at the GoLucky residence. Still, it's not too bad when your major decision of the day is whether or not to go see the Red Elvises at the Hurricane tonight. It's been a party weekend; in the Keys we aren't scared when the party goes into extra innings. Never caught Keys Disease, yet I don't like passing up a good time. Life is short. Eat dessert first.
Judging from the number of cars I saw at Crane Point on my way home from watching the Eagles victory at the Marathon Grille and

Ale House, Crane Point had a massive crowd for their event. The BTA Halloween party should be another serving of Big Time Fun. Chamber of Commerce weather is predicted and the volunteers have been working tirelessly to make sure the kids have a reason to smile. For those of you still scrambling to right the ship and keep from drowning, my heart goes out to you. Ask for help, your brothers and sisters are eager to throw you a life preserver if they have one that can help you stay afloat. I like staying home, but I also feel an obligation to go out and pump the few dollars I have to spare into my community. Over tipping is the new black, it's always in style. Stay Strong. I love you. ♥🖤

Happy GoLucky

Tuesday, 10/31/2017.

Happy Halloween, Y'all! Wimped out on the Red Elvises party at the 'Cane last night. The fun weekend caught up with me. Thankful that I made a special trip to KW to hear them last Thursday. This is a very special band. I want to hear them every time they make the trip to our islands.

Anybody else struggle with the decision on when to resort to antibiotics when combating a bacterial infection? Don't like being sick, but really don't like compromising my natural immune system

either. Damned if ya do, damned if ya don't. When will life start giving me easy questions? Okay, here's one I can answer without thinking . . . the answer is that IT'S GOOD TO BE ALIVE! Life can be sometimes tough, but always better than the alternative.
As my posts are less centered on recovery information, I sense my time on Facebook is coming to a close. If you want to stay in touch, P.M. me and we can exchange current contact information. Love Facebook, but for me it's best in small doses. BTA Halloween Party tonight should be the best ever. Stay safe and have fun. I'm batshit crazy about this town and everybody who lives here. Stay Strong. I love you. ❤🖤

The Gift of Tragedy

IRMA-GEDDON
NOVEMBER, 2017
Marathon, Florida Keys

Happy GoLucky
10/4/2017.
Each day I have less to say. I only write when I can't help myself, so I'm either gaining control or too tired to form sentences. Been a little held back by body ailments last few days. No need to complain, just keep on keepin' on and the sun rises every day. Each day is a miracle. I try not to take miracles for granted, but, yeah, I sorta havta or I spend all my time saying "WOW"!
A dear, life-long friend on the other side of the planet is having a tough time. Please say a prayer of healing if you will. Thanks.
Marathon High School Fighting Dolphins football team had an impressive victory in their last game of the season. Kids and coaches deserve big props for overcoming the many challenges they've year.

There's a free Insurance Claim Workshop today. https://www.facebook.com/events/166314613953491/

The more things get back to normal, the more apparent it is that there is a "new normal" in our town. At first, it was a big victory that roads were open enough that we could drive around the debris and get where we had to go. Almost two months post Irma, it's evident that we have some work left to do. BIG UPS to everyone who gets up every day and does what needs to be done. I'm just another soldier in this recovery army, but I salute all my brothers and sisters who show so much bravery, resiliency and resourcefulness each and every day. Hold your head up. We got this. Stay Strong. I Love You! ❤️🖤

Happy GoLucky

Sunday, 10/5/2017.

Been reading what y'all have written and posted here on Facebook. I'm reminded why I'm still here sorting through the garbage so eagerly most days. Between the "CLICK ME" bait and the "You're Politics Suck" posts, I learn about what real people are doing and feeling. Some examples:

Lisa M. is organizing another party at the Old Wooden Bridge in the Lower Keys. BIG LOVE to you, gurl.

https://www.facebook.com/groups/1148934105167465/…

Less happy, but of importance - Tammy Zalarick got her orchids jacked by some scum. Keep your eyes out and holler if you know anything about this. WE are the ones with the primary responsibility to protect our community. Our LEOs do a fantastic job, but they can't be everywhere.

https://www.facebook.com/…/114…/permalink/161845866154833 8/…

Sparky's Landing Lives!!! This has to be true because it has to be true. Matt and company did too great a job in KCB to just fade into the night. Grassy Key is alright and all but . . . this is really good news.

https://www.facebook.com/groups/1148934105167465/…

So, I broke down and started the course of Cipro. Should be restored to invincible in a few days. History tells me to jump on the probiotics starting now.

Eagles play at 1:00. See me at the Marathon Grille and Ale House. PLEASE don't buy me a drink. 😊;)

Hey Marathon, keep your head up. I'm loving you, hope you feel the same. Stay Strong. ❤️🖤

Happy GoLucky

Thursday, 11/9/2017.

It's recycling day in my neighborhood. We have this large blue bin on wheels that you put stuff in and leave in front of the house. When you go back later it's empty and your wine bottles, plastic shampoo bottles, tomato paste cans, and the other things you put in that bin are being trucked away, presumably to a fresh, new existence as something useful. Today felt like maybe I should have seen if I could fit in that bin and get a new start. That was before coffee. I'll be ok in a bit, but the beginning wasn't wonderful. One hard lesson I've learned is to forgive myself for occasionally hosting a pity party. I strive to be impeccable and strong. It's hard to accept that it's ok to slip now and then. There's enough sadness and misery in the world without dwelling on negativity. But it's a cruel man who can't manage to be kind to oneself.

Happy GoLucky
Saturday, 10/11/2017.
Picked up a Dawg at MIA yesterday. Not just anybody gets personal pickup service. The ride up left me thinking both how much has been done, and how much was left to do in the Irma recovery. Note that I was traveling AWAY from ground zero. Big reminder of the enormous size of this storm. There's an all day party benefit today for those folks hardest hit. Big Pine Flea Market. 10 a.m. to 10 p.m. You can do some good for your community and have fun doing it.
Taste of the Islands at Marathon Community Park tomorrow. Another good time that benefits us all.
Yesterday provided another BIG reminder - I don't like driving in Miami. It's just not fun, I guess you can get used to it. I don't intend to find out. Sitting on my rock is just fine with me.
Got home just in time to watch the sunset from Burdines. Southernmost Michael Q. joined us for a great Keys Casual dining experience. Always a pleasure to share time with good friends.
Well, me and the Dawg got stuff to do. Hope you enjoy today, the BEST DAY EVER! Stay Strong. I love you. ♥🖤

Happy GoLucky

The sun rises.
The sun sets.
Rinse.
Repeat.

***

Life will test you.
You never fail if you never quit.
Sing it LOUD!

The Gift of Tragedy

9 781978 442207